Apple Watch S

I0054129

The Simplified User Manual for iWatch Series 5 Owners

(The Simplified Manual for Kids and Adult)

Dale Brave

ISBN: 978-1-63750-182-5

Table of content

APPLE WATCH SERIES 5 1

INTRODUCTION 7

CHAPTER 1 9

APPLE WATCH GUIDE: HOW TO GET THE MOST FROM THE SMARTWATCH 9

WHAT CAN APPLE WATCH DO? 10

APPLE WATCH SETUP...11

HOW TO USE APPLE WATCH..12

RESET THE APPLE WATCH 13

THE VERY BEST APPLE WATCH APPS 13

TOP APPLE WATCH APPLICATION PICKS...14

CHAPTER 2 16

APPLE WATCH ACTIVITY AND WORKOUT 16

Apple Watch: Fitness and Activity Explained 16

Apple Watch: Workout Application..17

Apple Watch ECG Monitoring 19

Apple Watch Heart Rate Monitoring 20

CHAPTER 3 22

INCREDIBLE THINGS YOU CAN DO WITH APPLE WATCH SERIES 5 22

STAND ALONE FRIEND..22

SUSTAINING BATTERY LIFE 25

TIME FOR THE MAIN ONE BIG CHANGE..27

SHOWS YOU DIRECTION 29

SECURITY AND MORE...31

FEATURES OF APPLE WATCH SERIES 5 32

CHOOSE YOUR DESIGN...33

WHICH WAY TO GO?...34

THIS WATCH SCREEN IS ALWAYS ON..35

CHAPTER 4..38

DIFFERENCES BETWEEN APPLE WATCH SERIES 5, SERIES 4 AND SERIES 3 38

    Apple Watch Series 5 vs 4 vs Series 3: Software 39

    Apple Watch Series 5 vs 4 vs Series 3: Models 40

APPLE WATCH SERIES 5 VS 4 VS SERIES 3: HARDWARE 44

    Apple Watch Series 5 vs 4 vs Series 3: Design and display 47

APPLE WATCH SERIES 5 VS 4 VS SERIES 3: CONCLUSION... 50

CHAPTER 5 ....**53**

HOW TO USE THE APPLE WATCH EFFECTIVELY.. 53

    Utilize the Digital Crown to Navigate 54

    Utilize the Digital Crown to open up apps 55

    Use (customize) the application dock 57

    Keep Tab on Control Centre 58

    Improve Battery Life 59

    Walkie-Shareie.. 61

    Don't run out of data 61

    Select a New Watch Face.. 63

    Avoid Accidentally Changing the Watch Face....................................... 64

    Rename Your Apple Watch 65

    Avoid Screen Accidents with Water Lock 67

    Change volume on AirPods 68

    Practise Mindfulness with Breathe 69

    Use your iPhone to unlock your Apple Watch....................................... 71

    Use your Apple Watch to unlock your Mac... 72

    How to take Screenshots with an Apple Watch..................................... 73

    Use Your Apple Watch to hit your Fitness Targets................................. 74

    Share your Activity rings 77

    Take Photos with Your Watch.. 78

    Make your iPhone flash when pinging it.. 79

    Dismiss Notifications without removing them from Notification Centre. 80

    Let Shazam tell you all the music it heard today 83

    Control Spotify using Your Apple Watch 84

    Switch off the Apple Watch screen with Your Palm............................... 85

    Let Siri know when you've finished talking 86

Organise Your Apple Watch Home Screen 87

Setup the Watch on Your right Wrist (Lefties, pay attention) 89

Enable 'Prominent Haptic' for a pre-Announcement of Notifications 90

Answer Phone Calls on Your iPhone using the Apple Watch 92

Share Your Location from the Apple Watch 93

CHAPTER 6 95

APPLE WATCH GUIDELINES 95

Unlock Mac PC with Apple Watch 95

Add Music to the Apple Watch 95

Set alarm or timer 96

Use Apple Watch maps to navigate 96

Best Apple Watch faces 97

Update the WatchOS 97

Modular 97

Infograph 98

What's an Apple Watch additions? 98

Is the Apple Watch waterproof? 99

Is the Apple Watch appropriate for my Android? 99

Apple Watch and Siri 99

Can the Apple Watch charge wirelessly? 100

How do you add Watch face to the Apple Watch? 100

Will Apple Watch Monitor my Sleep? 101

Where is the Apple Watch battery indicator? 102

See Your apps, and Set up New Ones 102

How to add watch faces to the Apple Watch? 103

May I use Apple Pay on the Apple Watch? 104

Check Your Heart rate 105

How does Apple Watch's Fall Recognition work? 105

Will the Apple Watch hook up to Wireless Headphones? 106

Monitor your steps, and close the Rings 107

Read and Clear Notifications 108

CHAPTER 7 110

TIPS FOR APPLE WATCH SERIES 5 110

CHAPTER 8 116

 APPLE WATCH SERIES BEST FEATURES 116

Always On, Almost Perfect.................................... 116

Screen: Always-on is a large deal........................ 118

Compass: Maps made Better.............................. 120

WatchOS 6 Routine Monitoring: Easy and Private 123

Battery Life: Nightly Charging required 125

Design: Business as usual................................... 126

Apple Watch Series 5 and watchOS 6: Filled with improvements.......... 127

Introduction

Get Acquainted with your Apple Watch Series 5: iWatch Series feature you are never aware of!

This is a simplified guide with instructions to the shortcuts, tips, and tricks you should know about the new **Apple Watch Series 5**, and workarounds that will turn you into a guru in no time.

To make things simple, Author **Dale Brave** has exclusive tips and tasks you can achieve with your new Apple Watch Series. *He has also compared the Apple Watch Series 5 to Series 4, and Series 3 here, and that means you can see precisely what the variations and similarities are, whether you are looking to upgrade or take the smartwatch plunge.*

This simplified book will also get you equipped with

knowledge on how to take the maximum advantage of your *Apple Watch.*

Also; this book is simple enough to understand and a follow-through guide suitable for kids, adolescents, teens, and adults even if you are a beginner or dummy, seniors, or an expert in the computer and technology category.

This edition of *"The Simplified Manual for Kids and Adult- by Dale Brave"* book is suitable for kids, teens, adolescents, and adults who are either dummies or seniors interested in finding an accessible guide, manual and exclusive information on making the most of their Apple Watch Series 5: iWatch Series Tablets. You're in good hands!

Chapter 1

Apple Watch Guide: How to get the most from the Smartwatch

If you own an Apple Watch - or you're wondering what Apple's so-called iWatch does - you have the best smartwatch in the world available. However, there is a steep learning curve and getting the most from your Apple Watch and its selection of fitness, workout, and time-saving features, which is what this complete guide for Apple Watch is to accomplish. We've covered the essential questions and can help graduate you to a power user - covering top tips, essential applications, and stylish ways to make your smartwatch better still.

What can Apple Watch do?

It's one of the typical questions among people looking to purchase for the first time - what can the Apple Watch do?

Well, much more than only offering you the opportunity to read texts and answer phone calls on your wrist rather than your phone, which are the primary features everyone knows.

- Get emails and notifications on the wrist

- Fitness tracking

- Workout tracking

- Heart rate monitoring

- ECG monitoring (on Watch Series 4 and Series 5

only)

- GPS monitoring of exercises (on GPS variations)

- Make phone calls and receive communications from your telephone (LTE variations with a data plan)

- Turn-by-turn navigation

- Siri commands - alarms, timers, reminders

- Flash seat tickets and boarding passes

- Tell the time

Apple Watch Setup

When you take your Apple Watch out of the package, it's identical to everyone else's. Why is your smartwatch personal is the style and the apps, which means your

Apple Watch will be unique to your preferences.

1. Add your **Apple ID**.

2. Produce a **passcode**.

3. Install your apps.

4. Calibrate your activity configurations.

5. Manage your notifications.

6. Backup your settings.

How to use Apple Watch

The Apple Watch can be tough to split, and the first day can be considered a little frustrating for the uninitiated. Navigating selections and locating the information you are considering may take some time to get. Before very long, though, you will be using the digital crown, adding and using complications, changing watch faces and using **Apple Pay**.

As you read further, you will learn how to use the Apple Watch, including all the new features and user interface tweaks from watchOS 6.

Reset the Apple Watch

The Apple Watch is super secure, so whether it's lost or stolen, it can not be utilised without your permission, which means it needs to be correctly reset and unpaired from your iPhone before it could be added to a fresh one.

To achieve that, you will need to check out your Watch friend application on your iPhone and feel the unpairing process.

The very best Apple Watch apps

If there's one major differentiator between your Apple Watch and any competitor, it is the wide breadth of apps; just like the iPhone, Apple has remained the killer top features of the Apple Watch up to its multiplicity of developers.

Top Apple Watch application picks

- Strava

- Spotify

- ESPN

- CARROT Fit

- Streaks

- AutoSleep

- Just Press Record

- Citymapper

…among many others depending on your desired functions.

Chapter 2

Apple Watch Activity and Workout

Among the key top features of the Apple Watch is really as an exercise tracker and sports activities watch. The wonder of the smartwatch is adding this type of features into a unitary device - even though it's taken a while, the Apple Watch is a significantly powerful device.

Apple Watch: Fitness and Activity Explained

It's a good fitness tracker and can also monitor workout routines - and if you have a *series 5* with GPS navigation, it can substitute your standard fitness watch. The activity application keeps track of motion, calories burned and standing time, and you're encouraged to 'close the bands' to make your daily goals.

Gleam Breathe app, which stimulates mindfulness, and taking periods of your entire day. All stats are viewable on the watch, are monitored within the experience application on your iPhone, and populate the Apple Health app, too.

Apple Watch: Workout Application

The Workout application is a different beast and allows you to track a couple of different activities, from running and cycling to indoor workouts (which essentially track your heart rate, calories and time spent).

The Workout application now features:

- Indoor Walk.

- Outdoor Walk.

- Indoor Run.

- Outdoor Run.

- Indoor Cycle.

- Outdoor Cycle.

- Elliptical.

- Rower.

- Pool Swim.

- Open water Swim.

- Yoga.

- Hiking

Outdoor exercises are tracked with GPS, as the rest features; duration, heart rate, calories burnt and a lap feature. They are stored in the experience application on your iPhone to see back after, challenging maps and stats you'd expect.

The Workout application was treated to some other overhaul in watchO5, with automated run recognition added along with running specific additions such as Speed Alerts and cadence tracking, unlike many sports watches.

Apple Watch ECG Monitoring

Arguably, the largest addition taken to the Apple Watch Series 4 (and also available in the Series 5) was the ECG monitor; it'll track the tempo of your heart, looking for indicators of *a-fib (Atrial fibrillation)* - a disorder that is a leading reason behind strokes due to poor blood flow in human. Essentially, it's with the capacity of taking medical-grade readings of your heartbeat, checking for irregular activity and even letting you have a PDF report to show your physician.

Apple Watch Heart Rate Monitoring

So how exactly does apple watch monitor heart rate?

Heart rate monitoring has been an essential area of the Apple Watch, and since the manufacturing watchOS 4 that it has been turned into a robust tool; also the Apple Watch can utilize your heart rate in the following ways:

- Tracking resting heart rate.

- Taking live heart rate readings.

- Tracking heart rate during workouts and utilizing it to provide more accurate calorie burn.

- Alert user to abnormal or elevated heart rate.

- ECG readings (Apple Watch Series 4 and Series 5 only)

Heartrate activity is currently tracked during the day, and you can also track the heart rate while resting, which is a huge indicator of enhancing fitness, and even fatigue and stress. Also, the heart rate monitor will keep track of your ticker and alert you to an increased *bpm*, that could be dangerous.

Chapter 3

Incredible Things You can Do with Apple Watch Series 5

Apple creator Steve Jobs didn't wear a wristwatch, and according to an interview with **Jony Ive** (Apple's previous Chief Design Official), the theory for creating the business's first wearable didn't even happen until 2012. However, Apple loves and appreciates watches and, with each iteration, like the new Apple Watch Series 5, spent some time working to make it the best-selling wearable watch.

Stand Alone Friend

It's well worth reiterating that the *Apple Watch Series 5*

is also a great stand-alone digital friend; they have built-in *GPS*, and that means you always know where you're heading, they also have a *32GB storage* for your music, integrated *Apple Pay*, and, with respect to the model, mobile service for phone calls, textual content, and data (this usually costs approximately $12 per month extra on your mobile expenses).

Speaking of heading it alone, Apple Watch now has immediate access to the *App Store* on the watch; this feature wasn't available during screening, as it will be released with watchOS 6, meaning other Apple Watch models will also access the store.

Integrated with health monitoring is *Apple Watch's heart rate monitor*; therefore, I always know very well what kind of exercise, relaxing, and recovery heart rates I'm attaining. It's also viewing for abnormal and high heart rates, and there's a built-in electrocardiogram and ECG App. To utilize it, I make sure the watch is snug on my wrist, and after 30 secs I know easily if I have sinus tempo (good) or need to go to a doctor.

Apple Watch Series 5 is always ready for a swim and are designed for a gentle browse in about up to 50M of water. The Apple Watch Series 5 I tested, a 44 mm stainless model with a Milanese loop music group and cellular support, costs $799; nevertheless, you can purchase a 38mm GPS-only model with a sports music group for less than $399.

Cellular connectivity is nice to have, as will be the high-end materials, but I believe the 38mm Apple Watch Series 5 is a superb value, and also you still get the Always-On flash, map access, the compass and everything medical and activity features. Apple Watch

Series 5 doesn't invariably raise the pub for smartwatches but, with it, Apple has polished the already excellent wearable. I remain a fan.

Sustaining Battery Life

Keeping the *flash on* at all times naturally means the Apple Watch screen uses more battery life, but Apple mixed the *LTPO* tech with a fresh low-power screen driver, a far more energy-efficient force management integrated circuit, and a more ambient light sensor.

An advantage of keeping the **Apple Watch Series 5** from turning out to be a power-draining device is by maintaining it in a darkened theatre or supper spot; the sensor will pay better focus on its light environment, and I pointed out that it even muted the screen brightness in my living room where I'd dimmed the lamps to watch Television.

I've gotten accustomed to the sometimes-over-bright *Apple Watch* face after I first glanced at the now more tactful user interface, I used to be straining a little to view it; this is "my" problem, not "Apple Watch" problem. It wasn't a long time before I got used to the reactive Apple Watch Series 5 screen, I likewise have the choice of increasing the default flash screen brightness, though that may adversely impact my electric battery strength.

Apple will however, flourish in the effort to produce an always-on screen within an Apple Watch that lasts 18 hours about the same charge. I've worn the Apple Watch Series 5 the whole day without ever operating out of power before setting it back again on the wireless charging at night.

Time for the Main one Big Change

The Apple Watch Series 5 framework has not changed from this past year, except the Always-On Retina Screen, which has been the Apple Watch Series 5's most significant change; however, Apple Watch OS 6 offers lots of valuable improvements, but still, maintain the same design.

Now, Apple Watch's face will only come on when you raised your wrist, which had been a good move, allowing Apple to guarantee almost 18-hours of smartwatch electric battery life, however when I lower my wrist, the watch is changed into an inert little bit of metallic with a dark cup (or sapphire crystal) face. The Always-On screen is not only a "leave it on and hope battery life isn't terrible technology." I love how Apple thought this through by utilizing a mixture of technologies to keep the face lit and glanceable no matter what.

This past year, Apple introduced LPTO (Low-temperature poly-silicon and oxide) technology to its OLED Retina flash within its bigger flash (it also curved the corners).

It's LTPO, which allows the Apple Watch Series 5 to slow down its refresh rate from 60 Hz to at least 1 Hz (basically from 60 times per second to at least one time per second), thus giving it a much slower and less power consuming screen refresh rate. Because of this, the flash is only going to change for a scheduled appointment or important notification or only one time per minute. Regarding the Infograph watch face that usually has a second-hand cruising on the facial skin as it ticks off a few seconds, the second hands disappear in the Always-On setting and only changes at minute intervals.

The more apparent change in **"Always On"** mode would be that the white-coloured backgrounds turn black on some faces. In others, shiny colours go more muted. Apple modified all its watch encounters to work in *Always On setting*. Overall, the lighting diminishes with what is about 50 percent, and the effect is a wristwatch face that are relaxing but can be read even though I glimpse down within my wrist.

Shows You Direction

As I mentioned, one of the best Apple Watch features is its navigational features, driven by Apple Maps; the application is installed in the watch and can inform me exactly which path I'm facing. The user interface is similar to a physical compass in digital form, and swiping through; the interface provides my usage of more specific location details, including latitude, longitude, and floor elevation. I didn't have the chance to climb any mountains, but, based on the Apple Watch Series 5 compass, I'm at about 20 feet above sea level in my own home and, on the 8th floor of my office, about 80 foot above sea level. Access to this detail flash makes it feel just like I've tapped into a primary give away from the Apple Watch Series 5 detectors.

I liked the compass a lot, which i added, and it gives a little fine detail of additional information on a wristwatch face, like the time or your sessions) on my go-to watch face. Nobody will ever have the ability to point me in the incorrect direction again. There are always a couple of other exciting updates on *Apple Watch Series 5*; Siri now has Shazam-like features (while I listen to music, I could lift my hands and ask *Siri, "What's that track?"),* the smartwatch uses its mics to pay attention, and it correctly recognizes songs, even showing album covers.

Siri can also search the net and flash a summary of SERPs on the watch, so once I request for the capital of Texas, I got a perfect result (it's Austin). However, when I asked Siri showing me iPhone reviews, she explained to go surfing to discover more info about iPhone.

Security and More

There are a variety of new safety features that are almost impossible for me personally to test. The best is Sound; it can inform you of the current ambient sound level in decibels, and if the long-term use of it will harm your hearing. You can even set up the *Apple Watch Series 5* to warn you if you're in times (for lots of minutes) with ear-drum-damaging sound levels.

There's also the capability to make International

crisis/emergency phone calls through the watch in over 150 countries. Appears like a great feature I am hoping never to use.

Features of Apple Watch Series 5

A good move is to modify things as little as you possibly can, and lean into what people like, and fix small, petty issues yourself. Externally, the apple watch series 5 has the same size and form as the Apple Watch Series 4, but Apple has made a small number of changes which current (and future) Apple Watch followers will appreciate, as the most apparent is the always-on screen.

I've been using Apple Watches for a long time, and as much as I like them, I never knew I would so fall in love with the new feature of me reducing my arm, and the screen going completely dark. Real watches never switch off, even digital ones.

Choose Your Design

I never really had a problem with Apple offering matched pairings of the Apple Watch and music group, but many people thought they needed more options. An attribute Apple phone calls *Apple Studio room*, which enables you to choose your Apple Watch materials and bands individually for a genuine mix-and-match experience.

Also, it's well worth noting as the Apple Watch starts at $399 (GPS, only), you can easily crank up by choosing stainless, brushed titanium (which is lighter yet stronger than stainless), or even ceramic (which is gorgeous). If you'd like the option of the $199 Apple Watch, you'll need to return the still-available Series 3. It's a good product but won't have a compass or the new always-on screen feature.

Which Way to Go?

Being a directionally challenged person, I'm probably more worked up about the Apple Watch Series 5's new compass features and application than I will be. I love it when my watch can inform me not only the path of the North Pole but through the north. The Apple Watch will change for seasonal variants of the poles, which means you don't get "kind of" north; you get the real thing. The application itself is smooth and worked flawlessly in the demonstration space. I scrolled through to the Compass App flash screen and observed it also shows a sea-level altitude reading.

Certainly, the compass is a lot more useful when it's built-into other apps, like Apple's maps app. Now the Apple Watch map screen will have the same "which way am I facing" arrow as it can on the iPhone. Furthermore, third-party companies, like Yelp, can integrate the same arrow and that means you know which strategy to use to find that amazing Thai restaurant.

Apple didn't execute a great deal with the Apple Watch Series 5 security features but did add the power for the cellular types of the Apple Watch to dial crisis services (think 911 in the U.S. or 112 in Spain) in 150 different countries. So, if there is a fall in Cina, the watch can identify it and call local government bodies.

This Watch Screen is Always On

The Apple Watch Series 5 flash screen, automatically

switches from full lighting and color to a relatively dimmer light when you lower your wrist. What you'll then see is a mainly black background screen with lighter colors for elements you'd want to see; when you raise your wrist, the screen change back again to full color.

Behind the scenes is something called *low heat polysilicon and oxide (LTPO) screen*; in Always-On Setting, the LPTO changes the flash screen refresh rate from a far more power starving 60 Hz to at least one 1 Hz; because of this, the low-power always-on flash will, for example, only change once every second. When the always-on flash screen feature is enabled, it removes a lot of the white-color from most Apple Watch faces, but it doesn't remove complications; those features still show up, though they upgrade on the second-by-second basis.

AFTER I tried the new flash in the demonstration space,

I had been surprised at how well the flash screen switched from active mode to always-on mode by just me raising and lowering my hands. Apple also addressed one of my other Apple Watch frustrations: the too-bright flash in the darkroom; now, the ambient light sensor is continually scanning for different light situations, and you will be much dimmer in a cinema than it might be outside.

Chapter 4

Differences between Apple Watch Series 5, Series 4 and Series 3

The *Apple Watch Series 4* was announced in September 2018, but this product has been succeeded by the *Apple Watch Series 5*.

Apple Watch Series 5 smartwatch sits alongside the *Apple Watch Series 3*, while Series 4, Series 2, Series 1, and the initial Apple Watch are discontinued.

To make things simple, we've compared the Apple Watch Series 5 to Series 4, and Series 3 here, and that means you can see precisely what the variations and similarities are, whether you are looking to upgrade or take the smartwatch plunge.

Apple Watch Series 5 vs 4 vs Series 3: Software

- All will run WatchOS 6

- Extra features on Series 5.

The Series 3, Series 4 and Series 5 will all run WatchOS 6 when it arrives on 19 September, 2019, as will the Series 1 and Series 2, although the software is coming later for those devices. The initial Apple Watch will not support WatchOS 5, and it will not support WatchOS 6 either.

All generations, except the initial Apple Watch, therefore all provide a similar experience, even if there are many extra features on the Watch Series 4 and Series 5, like fall detection and the ECG function, as well as the Always-On Display and built-in compass on the Series 5.

With **WatchOS 6**, *an ardent App Store, woman health*

tracking, improved Siri, Activity trends, and more will all be arriving on Apple's smartwatch.

Apple Watch Series 5 vs 4 vs Series 3: Models

- Series 3: Aluminium only options, two colors, Nike+ model

- Series 4: No more available through Apple

- Series 5: Aluminium and stainless options (3 colors), Titanium options (two colors), Ceramic option (one color) Nike+ models and Hermès models

- GPS and Gps navigation and Cellular options for Series 3 and Series 5

- Size options: 38mm/42mm (Series 3),

40mm/44mm (Series 4 and 5)

When the initial Apple Watch was launched, its case was available in aluminum, stainless and special materials like solid platinum, which came in two size options of 38mm and 42mm. The Series 3 then launched a ceramic model, but this is discontinued when the Series 4 showed up. Ceramic is back again on the Series 5 though, plus a new titanium option.

The Series 3 is currently only available with an aluminium case, either silver or space grey, with a Sport Music group. You can of course buy individual straps, nevertheless, you won't be in a position to get the Series 3 in stainless or any other materials.

Apple Watch Guidelines

The Series 3 will come in 38mm and 42mm size options,

as well as with a selection of Gps navigation only or Gps navigation and Cellular. Gleam Space Gray aluminium Nike+ model available with an Anthracite and Dark Nike Sport Music group. The Nike+ model is also available in GPS and GPS navigation and Cellular options.

The Series 4 is no more available through Apple and with the Series 5 starting at the same price as the Series 4, we are moving straight onto the Series 5 models.

The Series 5 has much more possibilities than the Series 3 and it will come in 40mm and 44mm sizes. First of all, there is the typical Apple Watch Series 5, which will come in selection of three aluminium colors and nine standard Sport Music group options. You will find then stainless case options, also available in three colors, as well as various strap options from Sport Loop rings to the Milanese Loop and the Leather Loop. The titanium models come in two color options with multiple straps, and the ceramic model will come in one color option with various strap options.

Aluminium models come in Gps navigation and Cellular models, while stainless, titanium, ceramic and Hermès models are Gps navigation and Cellular as standard. You can also use Apple's new Apple Watch Studio room to pair in the Series 5 model you select with the strap you want. Previously, you'd to buy additional straps individually if you desired a different strap from what the model you selected came with.

There's also Series 5 Nike+ models available, all with aluminium casings, and Series 5 Hermès models available, which have stainless casings (two colour options) and special Hermès straps. While all the typical Series 5 models and the Nike+ models come in both case sizes though, a few of the Hermès models only come in either 40mm or 44mm, not both.

Apple Watch Series 5 vs 4 vs Series 3: Hardware

- **Series 3:** S3 processor chip, W2 wifi chip, Bluetooth 4.2

- **Series 4:** S4 processor chip, W3 wi-fi chip, electrical heart sensor, fall recognition, Bluetooth 5.0

- **Series 5:** S4 processor chip, W3 wifi chip, electrical heart sensor, fall recognition, built-in compass, Bluetooth 5.0

- **Series 3/4/5:** Barometric altimeter, ambient light sensor, built-in Gps navigation, optical center sensor, accelerometer, gyroscope, 802.11b/g/n 2.4GHz Wi-Fi, 18-hour electric battery life.

The Apple Watch Series 3 has a dual-core processor chip called the S3 under its hood, in conjunction with a radio chip called the W2. The Gps navigation only model has 8GB of memory space, while the Gps navigation and Cellular model has 16GB of storage, as well as LTE connection. The LTE online connectivity means you may make and receive phone calls and texts, as well as perform all the jobs you'd want to on your Watch without your iPhone in range.

Both GPS and LTE and Cellular Series 3 models offer Siri directly from the watch rather than transferring it to your iPhone, as they are doing on the Series 4 and Series

5.

The Apple Watch Series 4 and Series 5 come with an upgraded processor chip that is claimed to be 2 times faster than the S3, called the S4. There is also the next era cellular chip called the W3. Lots of the hardware features will be identical to Series 3, like the barometric altimeter, built-in Gps navigation, and the optical heart rate sensor; however, the Series 4 and Series 5 do put in a few extras. They enhance the accelerometer from up to 16 G-forces to up to 32 G-forces, plus they also add a power heart rate sensor to the Digital Crown; once we mentioned, that may allow users to consider an ECG themselves. You can read more about this in our independent feature. Both LTE and Gps navigation and Cellular models have 16GB of memory space too, and the Series 4 and 5 also offer fall recognition.

Series 5 takes things one step further still by supplying a built-in compass too, as well as international emergency calling.

Apple Watch Series 5 vs 4 vs Series 3: Design and display

- Series 3: 11.4mm solid, 5ATM waterproof, OLED Retina display with Pressure Touch

- Series 4: 10.7mm heavy, 5ATM waterproof, LTPO OLED Retina display with Push Touch

- Series 5: 10.7mm dense, 5ATM waterproof, LTPO OLED Always-On Retina display with Power Touch

- All straps compatible across all models

The Apple Watch Series 3 includes a solid rectangular

body with the Digital Crown and separate button on the right, plus a loudspeaker and mic on the left. It's water-proof up to 50-metres and it features Ion-X cup together with the screen. The Gps navigation and Cellular model is differentiated with a red accent on the Digital Crown.

The heartrate monitor is put on the lower of the watch body, combined with the release buttons for switching out the straps and the second-generation OLED Retina screen sits at the top, 2 times brighter than the Series 1 at 1000nits. The Gps navigation model has an amalgamated back, as the Gps navigation and Cellular model has a ceramic and sapphire crystal back too.

The Apple Watch Series 5 and Series 4 both sticks to a simple design and same strap mechanism as the Apple Watch models, which have eliminated before them, but Apple made a few changes with these models. First of all, the Digital Crown on Series 4 and Series 5 models has an electric centre rate sensor built into it, which is in addition to the optical cardiovascular rate sensor on the underside of the watch instances.

Apple Watch Series 5 Overview

The Series 4 and Series 5 likewise have a much bigger screen with rounded edges, making full use of the area available and producing a bolder design. The 40mm Series 4 and Series 5 provide a 759 square meters screen area set alongside the 563 square meters on the 38mm Series 3, as the 44mm Series 4 and Series 5 have a 977sqmm2 screen area set alongside the 740sqmm2 of the 42mm Series 3.

The larger screen ratio makes the Series 4 and Series 5 look quite dissimilar to the Series 3 despite an identical design overall. As well as the screen increase, the Apple

Watch Series 5 offers an *Always-On Retina screen*, which is the primary differentiating factor between it and the Series 4. The *Always-On screen* means you don't need to raise your wrist to wake the screen up, with the display always noticeable. The raising of the wrist or a tap on the screen will brighten the Series 5 screen instead.

Apple Watch Series 5 vs 4 vs Series 3: Conclusion

If you didn't spend money on the initial and you've decided the Apple Watch is currently something you want, purchasing the Series 3 on the new Series 5 model can save you £200, nevertheless, you lose out on some key features as well as your end options are more limited.

The Apple Watch Series 5 not only adds a far more advanced processor chip, but it includes a much bigger screen which makes better use of the situation size, a better accelerometer, fall recognition, Bluetooth 5.0, a power heart sensor, that allows users to measure their ECG (US/UK/Europe-only for the present time), as well as an Always-On screen and an integral compass.

The rest of the features might stay the same, but also for some, the new screen design, improved processor and ECG functionality, Always-On screen, and built-in compass may be the five features you needed to take the smartwatch plunge. For others, the Series 3 will more than suffice. In conditions of upgrades, people that have the initial Apple Watch, Series 1 or Series 2 will discover some important distinctions by switching to the Series 5, especially with the new display. People that have the Series 3 will also likely visit a good difference in the new model, but it could also be well worth waiting before Series 6 to find out if rest tracking shows up, or a big change up in design.

If you currently have the Series 4 and you're wondering whether to upgrade to the Series 5, you don't have to, until you want that *Always-On screen* function or the built-in compass.

Chapter 5

How to Use the Apple Watch Effectively

When the Apple Watch arrived in 2015, it wasn't simply a new product: it was Apple's first entry into wearables, a completely new market it had previously shied from. Unfortunately, without interface custom to attract on, this managed to get very hard for Apple to attain the same degrees of user-friendliness it experienced using its Macs and iOS devices.

Instead, Apple forged a new design program. You would find multiple control methods - a touch screen that's delicate to two examples of pressure, a button and a dial, and tone of voice control - and numerous third-party applications that take different methods to a user interface that took a couple of years to stay down; this means Apple Watch is filled with crucial features and unknown potential. In this book, you will learn tips and secrets to get more out of your watch, from essential interface ways to obscure tips for optimising how applications behave. And up-to-date regularly to include new features added in watchOS software improvements.

Utilize the Digital Crown to Navigate

When people first began to use the Apple Watch, they found themselves wanting a Home button like the main one below the flash screen on the iPhone and iPad. But there's already a home button: the Digital Crown. Pressing the Digital Crown performs activities like the Home button on your iPhone: touch it once to return to the house flash, or press and keep it to activate Siri.

Although there is not much in the form of multitasking on the Apple Watch, the Digital Crown can also allow something similar.

If you are using the Apple Watch and want to go back to the last application that was used quickly, double-tap the Digital Crown, and the last application will be opened automatically. (This also works from the clock face.) Then, once you're completed using that app, you can change back to the first app (which is currently the 'last-used app') by again double-pressing the Digital Crown.

Utilize the Digital Crown to open up apps

There are a variety of methods for you to navigate around the Apple Watch. You merely have to get the way that is right for you; for example, applications on the Home menu can be opened up by tapping the icon, but many people have discovered that tapping is inaccurate; sometimes you miss and open up the app left or right of your desired app.

To get the application in a crowded home flash screen, you may want to focus away using the Digital Crown to get the desired app. Once you have located it, tap near it to move on the region, and then centre the application on the flash.

Once it's centered, rather than tapping it, use the Digital Crown to focus it and open up it - it's a lot more accurate and carries a cool computer animation when zooming in to the watch face. On the other hand, try the alphabetical List View rather than the Grid View - this is simpler to navigate. Perform a hard-press on the home menu and select the appropriate option.

Use (customize) the application dock

The simplest way to open an application on your watch - or a popular app, at the very least - is to apply the dock, that was added with watchOS 3 and redesigned in watchOS 4. This fast-launching application picker is accessed by pressing the medial side button.

Any application can reside in the dock, whether or not it's preinstalled or created by an authorized user. Apps you place there are constantly refreshed, and that means you can easily see a live preview when you swipe laterally in the dock. Tapping on an application from its live preview will open it instantly.

You can choose up to 10 applications to put in the dock. Open up the Apple Watch application on your iPhone, then tap *My Watch > Dock*. Make sure favourites are ticked at the very top, then tap the *Edit* option at the top to move applications into or from the dock. You can even choose which order they come in. Additionally, tick Recents and watchOS woul automatically populate the dock with the applications you've been using lately.

Keep Tab on Control Centre

Swiping through to the watch face discloses Control Centre. You will see how much electric battery strength you have used; touch the percentage physique for quick access to Power Reserve if you want to conserve it.

There's also Airplane Mode, Cinema Setting (indicated by two masks - this stops the flash screen), silent mode, Do Not Disturb, a torch, a ping button for locating your phone, and an AirPlay button for hearing music from your Apple Watch with wireless headsets or a Bluetooth loudspeaker, and if you are utilizing a waterproof model (Series 2 or later) you will see water lock too, indicated with a droplet icon; this converts off the touch screen so that it isn't triggered by moving water in the shower or pool.

Improve Battery Life

How is your watch's electric battery performing? The initial and Series 1, when brand-new, could make it through one day's moderate use fairly easily: with careful use, they will make it through the majority of another as well.

Series 2, the best electric battery performer up to now, was best for two times useful between charges, and we discovered that it frequently managed to get to lunchtime on the third.

Series 3 and 4 have been similar to one. Five to two

times, although they rely heavily on how much you utilize cellular, which really is a battery killer.

If you are not getting these degrees of performance - and understand that electric battery life is one of the things that suffers most as a tool age - then it's well worth phoning Apple Support to find out if you have a duff model. But there are a few simple tricks you can test first.

It's possible that you need to check your use of precise, particularly power-hungry apps. Some watch consume more power than others; some configurations are better for enhancing battery life. Reducing notifications - and motivating your watch to check on, is using its combined iPhone for improvements less often - are well worth a try.

Walkie-Shareie

This application was added within the watchOS 5 updates, and we enjoy it - although we're yet to be convinced that it is a particularly practical feature. Still, it's free and for that reason, worth checking out for fun only. Open up the Walkie-Shareie application, and you'll see a list of individuals you can speak to. Touch the plus indication in the bottom to include more.

Now, from the app's main user interface screen, touch one of the yellow contact symbols to start speaking with them. Assuming they provide authorization (an one-off necessity), you can share instantly. Keep down the Chat button to chat; release to listen.

Don't run out of data

If you have bought the cellular-equipped version of the Apple Watch Series 3 or Series 4, you do not simply need to be concerned about the electric battery working out – additionally, you need to take into account your computer data limit.

You will keep a record of your computer data use and limit by logging into the **EE account** online or utilizing the **My EE** application for mobile. The application has one section for the phone and another for the watch. Many Apple Watch apps, both first- and third-party, will offer you ways to limit data utilization. Check carefully to see what your options are for the applications you prefer, and consider tensing data usage.

Finally, like the majority of streaming services, Apple Music runs on a lot of data. If you are approaching your regular monthly data limit, this can be a good application to stay away from.

Select a New Watch Face

Apple introduced three new watch encounters in watchOS 3: Numerals, a stunningly simple face with clock hands and, you guessed it, numerals; Activity, which places your rings front side and center on the screen in either analog or digital form; and Minnie Mouse to become listed on her pal Mickey. Various Toy Tale character types joined the team in watchOS 4, along with a stylish rotatable kaleidoscope face, while watchOS 5 added cool fire and liquid metal effects.

To add new encounters to your lineup, open up the Watch application on your iPhone and tap on Face Gallery underneath navigation pane. You can transform the order that will show up by tapping the **Edit** button next to *My Watch > My Encounters*.

You can customize that person (including its colours and

complexions), or you can swipe from left to right either left or directly on the watch screen to see more faces, in the order, you selected above.

Avoid Accidentally Changing the Watch Face

We've noticed from some individuals who find that they unintentionally change watch face without indication; this happens mostly in the shower, where, in fact, the warm water will often trick the watch into thinking it's being touched with a fingertip, with the effect that you emerge from the shower with lots of settings - perhaps like the selection of watch face - inadvertently changed.

But it is also easy to mistakenly swipe to a fresh face with all the touch screen for other activities.

If you're an exceptional shower personalized being, the

perfect solution is easy: start water Lock, this briefly deactivates the touch screen and therefore prevents functions or configurations being messed with by the meddlesome water, but if you merely use one face and would prefer not to need the watch change to others in error, you may as well delete all others from your My Encounters list.

Open up the Watch application on your iPhone and, in the **My Watch** tabs, touch on **Edit** next to **My Encounters**. Touch the red group next to the unwanted encounters, then tap **Done**. They're not gone forever - you can go into the Face Gallery anytime to retrieve them.

Rename Your Apple Watch

In case your name is David, for instance, and someone happens to obtain two Apple Watches, and you choose to keep these things both paired to the same iPhone at the same time, you might find yourself in the annoying situation of being unsure of which "David's Apple Watch" is which. Not that we're speaking from experience or anything.

One solution is by using a different face on each watch, but if you'd like to keep your favorite on both, a much better solution is to rename one of the watches to "David's Apple Watch Series 2" or, "Watchy Mc Watchface".

Renaming your Apple Watch is simply knowing how the option is strangely well concealed. Open up the Watch application on your iPhone, make sure you're in the **My Watch** tabs, then touch **General > About > Name** and *enter a fresh name*, then tap **Done**.

Avoid Screen Accidents with Water Lock

FOR APPLE WATCH SERIES 2 AND LATER ONLY.

As briefly discussed already, water Lock is a fresh feature, added in watchOS 3 with the improved water-resistance of the Apple Watch Series 2 at heart. It is rather handy (and turned on automatically) when you set to plan swimming regularly in the Workout app, but it is also smart to transform it by hand in the shower.

Swipe up from underneath of the flash to share the Control Centre, with a variety of popular controls. Tap the tiny water droplet icon.

To turn water Lock off again, rotate the Digital Crown dial. Water Lock will be deactivated, and you will hear a sound – i.e., the loudspeaker vibrating to drive out any remaining water. Water Lock is fired up automatically if you go to workout app. But if you begin another workout – such as a running - and then it begins to rain greatly, you can activate the feature from within the Workout app. Swipe in from the still left, and you'll start to see the typical options to pause or stop the workout, but there may also be a droplet icon to turn on water Lock carefully. The workout will continue; however, the touchscreen will be desensitized, so you will have to rotate the dial before using any onscreen functions.

We've never encountered rain sufficiently heavy to activate the watch's flash screen, but we do often utilize this feature whenever we run while wearing a jacket; it halts the sleeve from unintentionally pausing the workout, changing application or worse.

Change volume on AirPods

If you open up the *Now Playing* application on your

Apple Watch while using a set of AirPods, you can transform the volume using the Digital Crown dial.

To open up *Now Playing*, touch the medial side button, swipe to the right face and tap the application. If it's not in the dock you can transform this by starting the Watch application on the companion iPhone and heading to My Watch > Dock.

Better still, with certain types of watch it is possible to change the volume of the AirPods even if the flash is off. Open up the *Now Playing app*, then allow screen dim, and you will find you can change the dial and change the volume without activating increase to wake.

Practise Mindfulness with Breathe

watchOS 3 brought with it a new built-in application called Breathe. Its purpose is mindfulness: the application was created to show you through sleep classes, so you'll give more consideration to your mental health, which frequently gets the brief end of the stay when discussing wellness; you can as well customize this app on the Watch application, just pair your iPhone. Make sure you're in the *My Watch* tabs and then scroll down, and touch *Breathe*; from here, you can pick how often you want reminders to breathe each day (or switch off notifications entirely) and just how many breaths each and every minute is preferred. You can even adapt *Breathe's haptics*, the vibrations that will walk you through each session.

Apple's watchOS 5 series added a *Breathe watch face*, which you can access from the *facial Gallery* in the Watch application on iPhone. Tap to edit, and you could select from the traditional style, or new Quiet and Focus variations.

Use your iPhone to unlock your Apple Watch

Whenever you placed on your Apple Watch, you're prompted to enter your passcode to get access. Granted, it generally does not take lengthy time to tap in your passcode, but some individuals think it is fiddly, especially if you have one of the smaller-screen models. Fortunately, you have time to get accustomed to the workaround (I don't mean disabling the passcode, making things easier for thieves).

When you at first create your Apple Watch, you were asked whether you wished to unlock it, making use of your iPhone. If you have chosen yes, unlock your iPhone if you are prompted for your Apple Watch security password, and it will unlock your watch too. The procedure is manufactured even easier with *Touch ID* or *Face ID*.

If you didn't allow the setting at first but want to now, open up the Watch application on your iPhone and demand Passcode menu; from here, all you have to do is toggle the *'Unlock with iPhone'* option.

Use your Apple Watch to unlock your Mac

Apple's synchronicity between the devices arrived to play with watchOS 3 and macOS Sierra. Now you can use your Apple Watch to unlock your Mac computer, no security password necessary. First, ensure that your Macintosh and Apple Watch are both authorized into the same iCloud accounts and allow a passcode on your watch if you haven't already. On your own Mac computer, click through the following configurations: *System Settings > Security & Personal privacy > General.* Enable *'Allow your Apple Watch to unlock your Macintosh.'*

When you have two-step confirmation turned on, you will have to change to two-factor authentication instead, otherwise you will discover yourself jogging into a wall structure of frustration. You can view which security method you're using by putting your signature on into the *Apple ID* accounts.

To carefully turn off two-step verification and allow two-factor authentication, follow Apple's user guide.

How to take Screenshots with an Apple Watch

Going for a screenshot on Apple Watch - taking a static image of whatever's on the flash at confirmed moment, quite simply, which means you can share it or save it for future research. You can press the medial side Button and the Digital Crown at the same time, and the screenshot would pop-up in the Photos application on the matched iPhone, but because the start of iOS 10 and watchOS 3, Apple Watch screenshots have been handicapped by default.

If you wish to re-enable screenshots, open up the Watch application on the paired iPhone and tap **General**. Scroll down again and tap the slider next to allow Screenshots so that it turns *green*.

Now you can use the old technique: press the medial side button and Digital Crown at the same time, then try looking in Photos on the iPhone for the screenshot.

Use Your Apple Watch to hit your Fitness Targets

The *Activity app*, as its name suggests, tracks your exercise: the more you maneuver around, the more you increase your heart rate, and the less you take a seat on your bum, the better your progress towards three daily targets.

If you are finding it hard achieving your *fitness target*, you can always lower the prospective - it is the only one of the three that is user-customizable. If you are in the *activity app*, execute a company press on the flash screen, and you'll start to see the option to improve *Fitness Goal*; this will connect with today's target, and that means you can always lower the target in an 'about to lose out on an accomplishment' emergency situation. After all adjusting of your targets - there are many ways to burn off through those last few calorie consumptions before you go out of time. Most importantly, don't assume you must do a full-on workout or even go outside.

Relatively static activities could work quite effectively,

so long as you're active just a little and getting the heart going - we find practicing forward-defensives with a child's cricket bat curiously effective, presumably since it involves steps ahead, back, and exercising many areas of the body. Conversely, doing the football mini-game on Wii Sports activities seems much less effective, presumably because our foot hardly moves.

Jogging at that moment, provided it's reasonably vigorous running at that moment, happens to be our go-to approach topping up unburned calories by the end of your day; for the Stand total, be aware that just standing up for one minute isn't enough going to the mark for just about any given hour. You will need to go around just a little for the watch to note; walking right down to your kitchen and making a glass of tea should be enough, but there is that when cushioning across the house in socks or house slippers (especially on carpet), it sometimes does not grab the steps, or challenges to choose it up for some time.

If you are desperate going to the mark, you could put shoes on, or go and walk in your kitchen or jump along for a bit, but make an effort to understand that by sitting less you see medical benefits whether you win the 'game' or not.

Share your Activity rings

Activity-sharing on the Apple Watch gives you to see your friends' daily improvement in conference to their activity goals, from workout details with their rings. You can send positive messages to encourage a pal who requires a boost from the watch Activity app, or if you are feeling competitive, some prewritten snark is only a tap away.

Activity-sharing isn't fired up by default: you have to invite friends to share their data with you and await them to reply, i.e. in the iOS Activity app, not the iOS Apple Watch app - select the Posting tab underneath, then touch the + signal at top right. Enter a contact address, or search your contacts, then choose **Send**. They'll have to simply accept. If you are feeling particularly competitive (and also have updated to watchOS 5 or later), you can also challenge your pals to a competition.

Take Photos with Your Watch

Apple pre-installs a Camera application with the Apple Watch. That may seem unusual because no available Apple Watch model includes a camera of any sort; this app allows you to use the watch as a remote control shutter result in your iPhone camera; it's a useful feature to have.

Open up the Camera application on your Apple Watch, and it'll automatically open up the Camera application on the paired iPhone. Prop up the iPhone in a good vantage point (perhaps use one of the lovely iPhone camera tripods?) while looking at the shot is directly on your Apple Watch. If you are happy, you can touch the white group on the watch flash to have a picture or strike the '3s' button to employ a three-second delay.

Make your iPhone flash when pinging it

Now, this may be two tips for Apple Watch users that weren't already alert to a Find my iPhone style 'Ping,' that you can activate to find your iPhone. If you are at home and can't find your iPhone anywhere (we've all been there), you can merely gain access to the Settings Glance from your Apple Watch and tap the iPhone icon at the bottom of the flash screen; this will send a sign to your iPhone and make it 'ping' loudly, letting you easily think it is.

A convenient feature to have, right? But if you cannot find your iPhone by pinging it alone, touch and maintain the ping iPhone icon on your Apple Watch to activate the cameras LED flash as well, that may hopefully offer you a better notion of where your missing device is.

Dismiss Notifications without removing them from Notification Centre

When you get a notification on your iPhone, it's flashed on your Apple Watch - certainly. But did you see that once a notification has been dismissed on your Apple Watch, it is also dismissed from your iPhone's notification centre? Although it means you will keep your Notification Centre from becoming too cluttered, additionally, it may come as a drawback in relation to message notifications.

Say, for example, I get a WhatsApp message notification on my Apple Watch from my pal while I'm at work and can't answer him immediately. Easily dismiss the notification from my Apple Watch; it'll also dismiss it from my iPhone - however in doing this, I completely ignore that he has messaged me, and I finish up disregarding his message all night. Not ideal, could it be?

There's a straightforward workaround available, though - whenever you've received a complete screen notification you don't want to dismiss from the notification centre, press the Digital Crown to come back from what you were doing without removing it.

Quickly clear all Notifications

If you follow our previous advice regarding not dismissing notifications on your Apple Watch, one side-effect may be a big volume of notifications in your Apple Watch Notification Centre, available by swiping down from the watch face. Although we may not need to clear important communications/notifications, we don't want you to drown in a sea of irritating notifications either.

When you are in times like the main one described above, there are two possibilities for you: manually clear each notification by swiping left onto it and tapping *'Clear'*, or *clear all notifications* simultaneously. To clear all of your notifications simultaneously, gain access to the *Notification Centre*, and tap *Clear All*; this will clear all notifications from both your Apple Watch and iPhone.

Let Shazam tell you all the music it heard today

Apple depends on developers to generate alternative third-party apps to help make the Apple Watch experience as high as possible, and that's what the actual programmers of Shazam did. Just how many moments are you on trips and noticed a song that you want, but weren't sure what it was called? Shazam gives you the identification of the track you can hear right from your wrist - but that isn't all it can do.

From within the Shazam for Apple Watch app, force touch to share about a fresh menu. From here, you can select *"Start Auto Shazam"* that will constantly pay attention to your environment and identify any tracks that you hear as you start your entire day. Then, it curates that music into a playlist in Shazam; after that, you can export into Spotify.

Control Spotify using Your Apple Watch

The Music application for the Apple Watch is impressive, providing you full usage of your complete iPhone music library and permitting you to browse by song, artist, album, etc. However imagine if, like us, you do not use the stock Music application on your iPhone and instead use a third-party option like Spotify? There are still ways to get (limited) control of your music via the Apple Watch.

Instead of starting the Music application to gain access and control the music stored on your iPhone, first open up Spotify or any other very good music player on your iPhone and begin playing music. Once music is playing, press the medial side button on your Apple Watch to open up the dock and see *"Now Playing."* It appears similar to the Music app but gives you to regulate the music that's playing no matter where it's from.

You can pause, play, forward and back and control the volume from the Apple Watch.

Switch off the Apple Watch screen with Your Palm

Perhaps you have ever completed using the Apple Watch, reduced your wrist, and noticed the screen doesn't switch off? Even though it isn't an issue, and it will automatically switch off after a couple of seconds of inactivity, it'd be helpful to learn how to turn the screen off, right personally? It'd be great, particularly if you've handicapped wrist detection to save lots of battery. Well, you're in fortune, as there's a way to switch off the screen physically; and it's easier than you might think.

Once you have finished making use of your Apple Watch

and want to turn the screen off carefully, *place your hand on the screen.* Once you move your hands away, you'll spot the screen has switched off. They have other uses too - if you receive a telephone call on your Apple Watch, place your hand over the flash to silence the watch.

Let Siri know when you've finished talking

The usage of Siri on the Apple Watch makes difficult tasks like setting alarms much more straightforward to accomplish, by just telling Siri to create the alarm for you. It is also a fundamental element of the text messages app, being utilized to dictate your reply before transforming it to textual content prepared to send. But Siri on the Apple Watch continues to be young and has too much to learn - like when to avoid hearing your dictation.

We've discovered that when we've used Siri to dictate replies to text messages, it is not quite sure when to avoid hearing us and can begin to transcribe someone speaking near to you. However, we've discovered that tapping the flash screen after you've finished with your reply will minimize Siri from hearing and can transcribe what has been said.

It's not only helpful for dictation, though, as the sound clip may also be sent as a tone of voice mail via iMessage on the occasion that Siri doesn't transcribe accurately. Therefore tapping when you've finished speaking is practical, as you do not want to send your friend a tone of voice note with ten seconds of silence by the end, do you?

Organise Your Apple Watch Home Screen

It's wise to organise the applications on your Apple

Watch home screen. With the mixture of a little screen and a huge number of applications installed, it might become frustrating looking for apps that you would like to use.

Now, the fastest way to rearrange your Apple Watch home flash screen is to touch and contain the application icon until it wiggles, much as with the iPhone. Once everything begins to wiggle, you can pull the icon to its new position - it's also where you can uninstall any third party Apple Watch apps.

Additionally, there is another way to organise your Apple Watch home flash screen, namely utilizing the Apple Watch activity application on your iPhone. By starting the activity application and being able to access the App Design menu, you can get a synopsis of the design of your apps. From here, you can certainly rearrange them by tapping, keeping, and dragging them without having to be hindered by the tiny screen of the Apple Watch.

Setup the Watch on Your right Wrist (Lefties, pay attention)

Another tip is perfect for the lefties in our midst - sick and tired of wearing the Apple Watch on your left wrist? Tried it and didn't play well with the wrist-raising recognition? Don't get worried; you can change to your right wrist once you have tweaked your Apple Watch configurations in the Apple Watch partner application on your iPhone.

Once you have opened the app, navigate to *General > Watch Orientation*. From here you can select which wrist the Apple Watch will be worn on, as well as the Digital Crown's positioning. By selecting the right wrist and

Digital Crown positioning, it can help the Watch to learn when to awaken the screen as well as which way to orient the flash. Lefties have an option to make - you can either have the Digital Crown facing from your hands, or use it with the medial side button above the Digital Crown. Whichever you select, it doesn't genuinely have a lot of a direct effect on your experience with the watch.

Enable 'Prominent Haptic' for a pre-Announcement of Notifications

The decision to add a Taptic engine within the Apple Watch was welcomed with open arms by the tech community altogether. We've all got terrible encounters with traditional vibration motors - you've acquired your mobile phone on silent and are within an important conference when you receive textual content, however, the vibration is so noisy that each person in the area is aware you've just received a textual content. Haptic opinions isn't anything like this because of the Taptic engine, rather than feeling an enormous hype on your wrist when you obtain a notification, you'll instead feel a gentle 'tap' on the wrist to alert you. However, many people have commented that they hardly feel the haptic responses when they're on trips - *which tip is perfect for those people.*

Prominent Haptic is a pre-announcement vibration that's more powerful than the typical Apple Watch vibration to alert you of the inbound notification. To activate this, open up the Apple Watch friend application on your iPhone and get around to 'Seems & Haptics.' From here, you can customise the noises and haptic reviews of your Apple Watch, and toggle on the 'Prominent Haptic' feature. After that, you'll feel two vibrations once you get a notification - the pre-announcement vibration, and then your notification vibration.

Answer Phone Calls on Your iPhone using the Apple Watch

Even though we have been using the telephone feature of the Apple Watch, we missed this feature for several weeks. When you receive a call on your iPhone, you have the choice of responding to or declining the call, right?. You can find other possibilities: you have to use the Digital Crown to scroll down and gain access to them. The first option is to send an instant reply, that may disconnect the decision and make available to you pre-set communications such as "Can't speak, what's going on?" to send to the caller.

The next option, however, is a lot more helpful; even

though the telephone feature on the Apple Watch is cool, the loudspeaker isn't nearly noisy enough to have the ability to be utilized properly in a general public environment - it's just too silent to hear the call. So, in those situations you may use the Digital Crown to scroll down and choose *'Answer on iPhone'*; this not only answers the call on your iPhone but also places the recipient on keep until you have an opportunity to get the phone from your pocket/bag and unlock it; this negates any misunderstandings on the recipient's end, as they don't hear you rustling around in your handbag looking for your telephone.

Share Your Location from the Apple Watch

There is nothing more annoying than going to a meet-up with friends and family when they keep texting you to ask what your location is - particularly when you're using an Apple Watch and can feel every text on your wrist. You have a few options here: *ignore them*, activate *Do not Disturb* setting on your Watch or *show them where you are*. The latter appears to be the easiest option, but not when you're unsure of where you are, and that's where our last tip comes in.

All you have to do is open up the Messages application on your Apple Watch and choose a thread to answer, and rather than dictating an answer, touch the flash screen and choose *'Send Location.'* This will get your iPhone's current location and send it to everyone in the thread - which in this situation is all the friends you're off to meet. They can weight your location from within the Text messages application and easily see where you are.

Chapter 6

Apple Watch Guidelines

Unlock Mac PC with Apple Watch

If you are wearing your Apple Watch, think about unlocking your Mac without getting into your security password? Using PC Unlock, if you have paired your PIN on your watch (and you're putting it on), your Macintosh will open without a password.

Add Music to the Apple Watch

Be it managing downloaded music easier or streaming music directly from Apple Music as well as your wrist, the Apple Watch allows it. Remember, additionally, there is now also the official Spotify application for Apple Watch that you can dive into.

Apple Music allows users to stream and pay attention to a set of almost 30 million tunes, and today it's available on Apple Watch.

If you have an LTE-enabled Apple Watch Series 3, Series 4 or Series 5, you can stream music to your heart's content. You'll need a set of Bluetooth headphones.

If you are not rocking the cellular Apple Watch, you can also sync over albums and playlists and control music on your iPhone.

Set alarm or timer

The Apple Watch is, in the end, a wristwatch - so timekeeping is fairly on top of the agenda. Establishing timers and alarms is simple, especially if you utilize Siri.

Use Apple Watch maps to navigate

While Google Maps has been a slice from the system,

Apple Maps is an excellent experience on Apple Watch - with turn-by-turn directions and local sights.

Best Apple Watch faces

While Apple hasn't exposed the Apple Watch to the ravages of the third-party watch face market, the amount of options has soared with every new iteration.

Update the WatchOS

Maintaining your Apple Watch up-to-date means, you'll receive the latest features - like the ECG application, which launched as an over-the-air upgrade in December 2018.

Modular

With six complication places, the three icons in the bottom can be changed to common contacts, to allow you to make calls straight from the Watch. It will take calendar visits and flash the next engagement in the centre. A firm preferred.

Infograph

For the info obsessed, the Infograph supports eight complications, like the new corner placements; this employs the wider flash on the Series 4 and Series 5.

What's an Apple Watch additions?

In the watch world, a complication can be an added feature on the watch face, just like a dial that presents the date. Apple, in order to honor watch background, has used the terminology because of its smartwatches' widgets, which may be placed on a wristwatch face.

They could be used to show the weather, offer you news, show your battery percentage, launch applications, and more.

Is the Apple Watch waterproof?

The Apple Watch Series 3, Series 4, and Series 5 are waterproof up to 50 meters, meaning they may survive a drop in the pool, and you don't need to remove it in the shower.

Is the Apple Watch appropriate for my Android?

Android phones aren't appropriate for any Apple Watch. The minimal requirements are for an iPhone consumer who has an iPhone 5 or later working with at least iOS 8.2.

Apple Watch and Siri

Aside from Alexa - you could have Siri on your wrist wherever you decide to go. Siri requires a lot of work, but use our tips and you may take the benefit of everything it provides.

The easiest way to wake Siri is to carry down the Digital Crown - once you do so for two seconds, the listening indicator will pop up and you will release.

You can even now raise your wrist to the mouth area - and the listening indicator should appear. Ensure it's allowed in *Configurations* > *General* > *Siri* > *Increase to Speak.*

Can the Apple Watch charge wirelessly?

The Apple Watch cannot charge wirelessly - all Apple Watch models charge through Apple's proprietary magnetic charging dock system. However, the Apple Watch doesn't officially comply with the Qi Wireless Charging standard, as the latest iPhones do.

How do you add Watch face to the Apple

Watch?

1. Decide on a watch face that already has problems that you should edit.

2. Following that, keep down the flash screen on your Watch, faucet which green container you want to edit, and use the Digital Crown to scroll by which options you want on that person.

3. Press the Digital Crown again to save lots of the complications as well as your watch face.

Will Apple Watch Monitor my Sleep?

The Apple Watch can't natively monitor sleep. Likely because of the Watch's limited electric battery life, Apple is yet to start an official sleep monitoring app. However, there are always a sponsor of third-party Apple Watch sleep tracking apps on the App Store that would serve the purpose for which you need it.

Where is the Apple Watch battery indicator?

Similar to ways to swipe along through iOS, watchOS also gives you to get this done to gain access to certain settings of the Apple Watch. If you swipe up, you'll notice a percentage icon on the left side, below the Wi-Fi tab, and next to the Ping iPhone tab. Unless you fancy swiping each time you want to check on your electric battery, you can install the battery widget on customisable watch faces.

See Your apps, and Set up New Ones

Press the Digital Crown to visit a overview of all applications installed on your Apple Watch. These symbols will contain pre-installed applications from Apple and any applications which you have on your iPhone that are also appropriate for the Apple Watch.

That is a choice when you initially setup your Watch, but if you're looking for an application and can't think it is, or want to eliminate apps, then check out the Apple Watch application on your iPhone and scroll right down to the Installed on Apple Watch list. Touch each option to see settings on either deleting or setting up the application on your Watch.

To find new applications for your Watch, open the Apple Watch application and choose the App Store from the set of options at the bottom of the flash screen; this goes to a version of the App Store with all the current apps designed for your Watch, eliminating the guesswork from using the primary App Store application to see them. The applications you install will demand the same application to be installed on your iPhone too.

How to add watch faces to the Apple Watch?

You can add faces to the Apple Watch by going to the Watch application on your iPhone and hitting the facial Gallery tab at the bottom of the flash. Here, you can select from a variety of faces, which you can then personalise with problems (such as your electric battery percentage, or a shortcut to Strava) through the Watch itself. You can even edit which watch encounters show up through the My Encounters portion of the app.

If you wish to add something from your Photos, add it to the Favourites album. Once done, it'll show up for syncing in the facial Gallery portion of the app.

May I use Apple Pay on the Apple Watch?

Whichever Apple Watch model you have, double-tapping the medial side button, provides up your cards, and a tap of the reader enables you to use **Apple Pay** on these devices.

Check Your Heart rate

That is easy; press the Digital Crown showing the app screen to check out the heart icon. Touch it, and the Watch immediately begins taking your heart rate. A graph near the top of the flash shows your heartrate background. Twist the Digital Crown showing other screens, wearing down your heart rate data into relaxing and walking sections.

One thing to keep in mind is to ensure the Apple Watch is securely on your wrist. If it's loose, the dimension might not be accurate.

How does Apple Watch's Fall Recognition work?

The Series 4 and Series 5 are both outfitted with fall detection. If it detects a difficult fall, it'll hype your wrist and sound an alarm. It'll list fast access to Emergency SOS with a swipe gesture, that will contact emergency services. It'll also provide a button that says "I'm OK" unless you need help.

In case your Apple Watch detects a fall and then detects you've been immobile for one minute, it starts a 15-second countdown while tapping you on the wrist and sounding an alarm. The security alarm are sure to get louder and louder to attempt to alert another person to your preferences. It'll also automatically contact emergency services, providing where you are.

Will the Apple Watch hook up to Wireless Headphones?

The Apple Watch may use Bluetooth for connecting to wireless earphones. To take action, go to the 'Settings' portion of the Watch, before selecting 'Bluetooth' and these devices you are looking to set. We've found some problems with the Watch pairing to headsets that already are recognized to the iPhone, but it has assorted depending which earphones we have been using.

Monitor your steps, and close the Rings

Your Apple Watch is a thorough fitness tracker. We recommend establishing Apple Health on your iPhone to get the most out of your Apple Watch's fitness tracking features. Once you have, press the Digital Crown and look for the icon that looks like three rings - blue, green, and red - and tap it. The three rings represent your daily activity goals - movement (red for calorie count), exercise (green for movement), and standing (blue, with a target of standing once per hour).

Scroll down the flash screen to see your step count, distance walked, and the volume of stairs climbed. The task is to "close the Rings" by completing each different activity on a regular basis. Check Apple Health on your iPhone for more data, or go directly to the Apple Watch application and choose Activity to see more. If you're focused on using the Apple Watch as an exercise tracker, then decide on a Watch Face like Activity Digital or Activity Analogue to see your progress on screen all the time.

If you are using the Siri watch face, then the activity is shown permanently, or on encounters like Infograph, activity can be shown as a problem.

Read and Clear Notifications

When it's linked to your mobile phone, or if it's the 4G LTE version, the Apple Watch will screen message, email, and application notifications. To find out these, you swipe down on the screen. Notifications come in a scrolling list, and a tap will show all the available relationships. You can answer text messages using quick reactions, like tweets, and use your tone of voice rather than typing out a contact, for example. To make sure notifications stay useful, it's beneficial to clear out more information on them. Clear them separately with a swipe left, or press and contain the flash to get a *Clear All* option.

Chapter 7

Tips for Apple Watch Series 5

1. *Measure surface angles*

Series 5 has a compass sensor. Exactly like on iPhone, the Compass application takes benefit from it for a useful level feature. Just scroll down in the application to access this tool, then layout your watch on any surface to measure both its horizontal and vertical levels.

2. *Enhanced directions in Maps*

Like on iPhone, Apple Maps uses the built-in compass sensor to point the path you're currently facing, which will come in handy when working with step-by-step directions.

3. *Cover private stuff with all the always-on display*

The largest new feature of Series 5 is its *always-on screen* that enables you to tell time discreetly and look into other information shown on the watch face while in a gathering or training and never have to flip over your wrist. Fortunately, you may even choose to cover any delicate information from the prying eye whenever your wrist is down.

Begin by firing in the Watch application on your iPhone, then tap My Watch → Lighting & Textual content Size → Always On and turn the toggle Cover Sensitive Problems to the OFF position. Doing this will conceal any problems that screen private data whenever your wrist is down, including Calendar visits, Mail messages as well as your heart rate.

4. *Delete indigenous apps*

watchOS enables you to delete stock applications from the home screen much like iOS devices. Let's pretend you'd like to eliminate Apple's stock Information app - touch and keep its icon on the home screen, then strike "x" and verify the action by tapping *Delete App*. Don't worry; you can redownload erased stock applications by searching to them in App Store.

5. *Utilize dual the storage*

Series 5 doubles the inner storage over the predecessors from 16 to 32 gigabytes. Allowing you to retain more content on these devices itself, from applications to your preferred photos to Apple Music playlists, songs and albums, and beyond. This will come in useful if you don't have an LTE watch so streaming via cellular isn't a choice.

6. *Reorder your watch faces*

Like before, you can still edit watch faces on the watch itself or via the Watch application on your iPhone, However now, watchOS 6 also enables you to reorder them to your liking - press and hold the watch face to enter *Edit mode*, then drag the watch face to a new position. It'll be right there the next time you swipe through your watch faces.

7. *Choose any band you want*

Finally, you are no more confined to Apple's mixtures of Apple Watch bands and case materials. With Apple Watch Series 5, you can mix and match bands and cases materials any way you like, whether in store or online.

8. *Noise app*

Make sure to browse the Noise application (and put a

Noise complication on your preferred watch face) if you'd prefer to be alerted about contact with noise levels that could harm your hearing. This feature may decrease battery life, so utilize it sparingly, and only once it seems sensible (as in, you don't need a Noise complication on your nighttime watch face).

9. *Track your heart function*

As with Series 4, Series 5 includes an electrocardiogram that could save your valuable life by spotting adverse heart rate results even if you're unacquainted with them, such as whenever your heart rate is accelerating a great deal while you're not necessarily doing anything physically demanding.

10. *Finding iPhone at night*

That is an oldie, but goldie. Once you talk about *Control*

center and tap the telephone icon, the watch will ping your misplaced iPhone via Bluetooth or Wi-Fi. But if you touch and keep that same *Control center* toggle, doing this shall make your telephone flash. That's relatively great if you have no idea where your telephone is or want to find it at night!

Chapter 8

Apple Watch Series Best Features

Always On, Almost Perfect

It's quite easy to glance at the watch to start and see the time; I do it subconsciously countless times each day, even easily don't have a complete schedule of conferences and events. However, in an ironic twist, checking time was one thing Apple Watch wasn't everything helpful for - at least before the release of the $399 Series 5, out now; previously, the watch's face remained dark until you raised your wrist. The Series 5's watch face is always on, so whenever I glimpse down within my wrist, regardless of what position it's in, I could see what time it is.

It sounds a little silly, that Apple Watch is now able to

tell you time on a regular basis, and perhaps it is; but alongside the *heart health diagnostic tools* that made the Series 4 so essential, an integral *compass* and the *watchOS 6* features that improve almost every area of the Apple Watch experience, the Series 5's always-on screen makes the Apple Watch's place as the best smartwatch you can purchase.

Apple at first didn't declare a sleep-tracking feature for the Apple Watch when the Series 5 continued sale, but an unintentionally released screenshot for the Apple Watch Alarms application, shows a rest feature that hasn't been launched, yet it's unclear if the feature will debut, and what impact it has on electric battery life.

Apple Watch Series 5 price and availability

The Series 5 is open to online purchase starting from $399 (£399) for small aluminum 40-millimetre model with Gps navigation; for a supplementary $100, you can splurge on the cellular-enabled watch (which also takes a regular monthly data plan from your cellular carrier for yet another cost). The bigger 44-mm watch is $429, and $520 with LTE.

If you'd like something that looks and feels a bit more high-end than aluminum, the stainless Series 5 begins at $699, and the new titanium model is $799. If you feel like balling out, the white ceramic special release is back again for $1,299. The Series 5 replaces the Series 4, which is no more available through Apple but are available for a steal from third-party retailers. Apple continues to be offering the 2-year-old Series 3 for $199.

Screen: Always-on is a large deal

I've used another smartwatch on the marketplace, and the majority of them have always-on shows, but that means you can always start to see the time; however, apple's version of the always-on screen is just a little extra. The Series 5 doesn't merely demonstrate what time it is. When inactive, the screen shows you a dimmer version of all information on your watch face. I use the Infograph Modular watch face, which includes six complications combined with the time; therefore i get access to my most-used applications (Workout and Communications) as well as items of information like the elements and electric battery percentage. I could still see all that when the screen dims.

The difference is even starker with brighter watch faces like Meridian, which includes an almost completely white background that dims to black when you lower your wrist. The flash's ambient light sensor can identify how bright your environment is and change itself accordingly; therefore, the screen is never too bright or too dark.

When you're using an app, the *always-on screen* dims and blurs the backdrop showing you enough time when it's inactive; this pertains to all the Workout app, which still shows all your metrics even though you're not positively taking a glance at the watch. The only difference is enough time elapsed, which refreshes every second rather than counting milliseconds; this feature is extremely useful while operating because I no more have had to raise my wrist to see my speed or time. Even in bright morning daylight, I had formed no problem viewing my stats on the darkened screen. To save electric battery, you can change the always-on part off (open up the watch's Settings application and toggle it off under Screen & Lighting).

Compass: Maps made Better

I would have yawned when Apple announced that one of the headlining features in Series 5 is an integral compass; it just didn't excite me what sort of FDA-cleared ECG application did when the Series 4 was announced this past year. But I recognized precisely how useful the Compass application could be.

However, the compass isn't the only application that takes benefit of the watch's built-in magnetometer. Apple is starting the Compass API to third-party apps, and it is also utilizing it in its Maps app to allow a feature that presents to you which path you're facing. This is incredibly useful when i parked at the bottom of Runyon Canyon Recreation area, and had to determine which trail to consider. Maps consistently demonstrated to me which path I had been on, and what distance into the recreation area I used to be, which helped me realize after i needed to slice the hike brief and return.

I could see this feature being even more essential when camping or hiking in more remote control areas. Thinking back again to a time I acquired lost trekking in Sedona as a teenager in the pre-smartphone area, this feature would've been a life-saver. (Not actually for me - I survived - but also for another person.)

It ought to be noted that one watch rings will hinder the Series 5's built-in magnetometer. Essentially, any music group with a magnet in it'll toss off the compass's capability to execute, so if you're moving out for an experience, leave the Milanese Loop or Modern Buckle at home.

WatchOS 6 Routine Monitoring: Easy and Private

Apple isn't reinventing the steering wheel with Cycle Monitoring, but the truth that women are now able to track intervals on the best smartwatch on the marketplace, in addition to all or any of the other features which make it great, is a welcome change. I've used similar features from Fitbit and Garmin, and the features are the same. You self-report your intervals to start, and then your watches can begin accurately predicting when another one will start. I'm still in the first phases of using the Apple Watch's Routine Tracking app; therefore, i haven't examined out its predictions or notifications, but I appreciate the amount of detail I'm in a position to enter as it pertains to period movement, symptoms, and spotting. You can even add information regarding ovulation test outcomes, cervical mucus quality and basal body temperature in the iPhone Health app, and invite Cycle Monitoring to predict your fertile windows if you would like to use the application to plan or prevent being pregnant.

To begin with period-tracking, you'll need to insight your details in the iOS Health app, including details like the first day of your last period, amount of your routine, and typical period length. You'll be able to start logging your period in the Routine Tracking application on the watch, and even add the application as a problem on the watch face for easier access; i intend to keep it as a problem within period cycle, and then swapping it out for another application.

After a Privacy International study demonstrated that popular period-tracking applications might be seeping information about your health and sex to companies like

Facebook, Apple's on-device, hands-off method of health data makes its version of the feature even more compelling.

Battery Life: Nightly Charging required

I wear my Apple Watch from time I am awaken to work through each day 'til time I remove it to go to bed - usually around 16 hours per day. Old watches, especially the Series 3 and Series 4, could last a lot longer than that, but I never used them to monitor my sleep; therefore, i charged them every evening.

The Series 5's always-on screen doesn't appear to be a lot of an electric battery drain - at least less than the Series 3's cellular connectivity was when that watch debuted. After an entire 14-hour day of placing the new watch through demanding activities to test, including installing apps, trying out Maps and Compass, logging my routine, requesting Siri various questions, and monitoring a 3.75-mile run and a 2-mile hike as individual workouts, I had been down to 10%, and I hardly ever use my watch that intensively; I've stopped charging my Apple Watch daily, and i wish I possibly could squeak by on two times.

Rival smartwatches from Samsung (Fitbit and Garmin) offer multi-day electric battery life, but those watches also aren't as fully presented as the Series 5; for the present time, it's still a trade-off.

Design: Business as usual

The Series 5 appears similar to Series 4 in a single way. Apple introduced a fresh titanium finish, which is lightweight to slide on and looks stylish personally and cut back the white ceramic edition, which is a premium watch with a cost tag ($1,299) to complement.

The classic aluminum version continues to be the main one most people will buy. And Apple is currently letting you customize the watch finish and music group before you get, instead of needing to take whatever will come in the box and then selecting the strap you want.

Apple Watch Series 5 and watchOS 6: Filled with improvements

You don't need a string 5 to get among the better new Apple Watch features. One of the major things I love about using the Series 5 is the latest software, watchOS 6, which is available as an over-the-air update for the Series 3 and 4, too.

The best new features are the new Routine Tracking application for logging period circulation and symptoms (more on that in a moment), the Calculator app, that may save relationships with an integral suggestion calculator, the Noise application for monitoring decibel levels and the new independent Watch App Store. And that's not half of the improvements Apple shipped in this release. There's too much to love about watchOS 6.

I'm not amazed it took such a long time for a Calculator application to reach on the watch, considering that the iPad still doesn't have a local version, but I would never use my iPhone's calculator again. The watch app's suggestion calculator is a God-send, especially because you can modify the percentage and determine how much each individual owes for an organization dinner. When you have a few beverages and neglect how to do mathematics, the Apple Watch will perform the task for you.

The Watch App Store could very well be the most apparent gamechanger because you no longer require to set up watch applications from your iPhone. Which means that app designers don't have to produce iOS applications first and then make watch extensions, that ought to make watch applications more useful and specific. I question when Apple allows Apple Watch purchasers to create the watch lacking for any iPhone, too, which is currently the largest thing keeping the watch from being truly a completely impartial device.

www.ingramcontent.com/pod-product-compliance
Lightning Source LLC
Chambersburg PA
CBHW071709210326
41597CB00017B/2402